W9-BQZ-211

RECEIVED
NOV 01 2010
By_____

HAYNER PUBLIC LIBRARY DISTRICT
ALTON, ILLINOIS

OVERDUES .10 PER DAY, MAXIMUM FINE
COST OF ITEM
ADDITIONAL $5.00 SERVICE CHARGE APPLIED TO
LOST OR DAMAGED ITEMS

HAYNER PLD/ALTON SQUARE

# The GROSS AND GOOFY Body

# Moving and Grooving

## The Secrets of Muscles and Bones

By Melissa Stewart

Illustrated by Janet Hamlin

mc Marshall Cavendish Benchmark

New York

THIS BOOK WAS MADE POSSIBLE,
IN PART, BY A GRANT FROM THE
SOCIETY OF CHILDREN'S BOOK WRITERS AND ILLUSTRATORS.

Text copyright © 2011 Melissa Stewart
Illustrations copyright © 2011 Marshall Cavendish Corporation

Published by Marshall Cavendish Benchmark
An imprint of Marshall Cavendish Corporation

All rights reserved. No part of this publication may be reproduced, stored in a retrieval system or transmitted, in any form or by any means, electronic, mechanical, photocopying, recording, or otherwise, without the prior permission of the copyright owner. Request for permission should be addressed to the Publisher, Marshall Cavendish Corporation, 99 White Plains Road, Tarrytown, NY 10591.
Tel: (914) 332-8888, fax: (914) 332-1888.   Website: www.marshallcavendish.us

This publication represents the opinions and views of the author based on Melissa Stewart's personal experience, knowledge, and research. The information in this book serves as a general guide only. The author and publisher have used their best efforts in preparing this book and disclaim liability rising directly and indirectly from the use and application of this book.

Other Marshall Cavendish Offices:
Marshall Cavendish International (Asia) Private Limited, 1 New Industrial Road, Singapore 536196 • Marshall Cavendish International (Thailand) Co Ltd. 253 Asoke, 12th Flr, Sukhumvit 21 Road, Klongtoey Nua, Wattana, Bangkok 10110, Thailand • Marshall Cavendish (Malaysia) Sdn Bhd, Times Subang, Lot 46,
Subang Hi-Tech Industrial Park, Batu Tiga, 40000 Shah Alam, Selangor Darul Ehsan, Malaysia

Marshall Cavendish is a trademark of Times Publishing Limited

All websites were available and accurate when this book was sent to press.

Library of Congress Cataloging-in-Publication Data
Stewart, Melissa.
Moving and grooving : the secrets of muscles and bones / by Melissa
Stewart.
p. cm. — (The gross and goofy body)
Includes index.
Summary: "Provides comprehensive information on the role bones and muscles
play in the body science of humans and animals"—Provided by publisher.
ISBN 978-0-7614-4166-3
1.  Musculoskeletal system—Juvenile literature.  I. Title.
QP301.S835 2010
612.7—dc22
2008033557

Editor: Joy Bean
Publisher: Michelle Bisson
Art Director: Anahid Hamparian
Series Designer: Daniel Roode

Photo research by Tracey Engel

The photographs in this book are used by permission and through the courtesy of:
Cover photo: Jose Luis Pelaez/Getty

The photographs in this book are used by permission and through the courtesy of: *Alamy*: WoodyStock, 13 (top); Visual&Written SL, 13 (bottom); imagebroker, 17; PhotoStockFile, 18 (left); Colin Keates, 21; Stephen Roberts, 28. *Getty Images*: 3D4Medical.com, 4, 14, 33, 39 (left); Leroy Simon, 5 (top); Brandon Cole, 5 (bottom); Guillermo Hung, 6; Nucleus Medical Art, Inc., 11 (top), 22 (right); Raphael Van Butsele, 12 (bottom); Beto Hacker, 15 (bottom); Georgette Douwma, 16 (bottom); Justin Sullivan, 16 (top); Oliver Brachat, 22 (left); Ty Milford, 23; Ken Chernus, 24; Steve Wisbauer, 26; Superstudio, 27; David Deas, 29 (left); Tripod, 29 (right); MICHAEL KAPPELER/ AFP, 30 (right); Joel Sartore/National Geographic, 30 (left); Joe McDonald, 31 (top); Belinda Wright, 31 (bottom); SIU, 32 (left); Kallista Images, 34 (right); Girl Ray, 36; Camille Tokerud, 39 (right); David Waldorf, 40. *iStockphoto*: Brenda A. Carson, 11 (bottom). *Photo Researchers*: Peter Gardiner, 35. *Shutterstock*: Emin Ozkan, 7 (bottom).

Printed in Malaysia (T)
135642

J612.7
STE.

b19367545

# CONTENTS

# MARVELOUS MUSCLES, BRILLIANT BONES

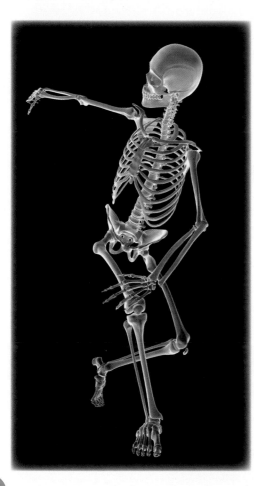

Your body has more than 650 muscles and 200 bones. How many of them are you using right now? Probably more than you think.

It takes twenty different muscles to smile and more than forty to frown. For a simple stroll down the street, you need more than two hundred muscles and at least one hundred bones.

Whether you're standing up tall or kicking a ball, scratching your ear or shaking your rear, winking your eye or zipping your fly, your body's muscles and bones control every move you make. And that's not all they do. You'll be amazed at all the ways bones and muscles make life better for you—and for other animals, too.

b193(7647)

Caterpillars don't have bones, but they use more than four thousand rippling muscles to wriggle along.

Why does a bird weigh three times less than other animals its size? It has lightweight bones. That's one reason it can soar through the sky.

The hagfish is a gruesome hunter. It uses its strong tongue muscles to bore holes into other fish. Then it eats the helpless victims from the inside out.

# MAKING A MOVE

You move the bones and muscles in your arms hundreds of times every day. But have you ever stopped to wonder how they work? Here's your chance to find out.

Pretend you're throwing a ball. As your forearm swings forward, two long bones inside act like a **lever**—a rigid bar that turns around a pivot point (your elbow).

The force that moves your bones comes from energy produced in your muscles. Where does that energy come from? Your cells make it. As blood flows through your body, it picks up **nutrients**

The energy you need to work and play is made inside your cells.

from your **intestines**. It collects **oxygen** in your lungs. Then it delivers these materials to your muscles and other body parts. When they mix inside your cells, they produce all the energy you need to live and grow and move.

## Mighty Muscles

If all the energy your muscles exert in one day were concentrated in your arms, you'd be able to lift two elephants high above your head. Now that's incredible!

## Did You Know?

More than half of all American kids break a bone before their eighteenth birthday. Luckily, young bones heal fast. If you break your wrist, it'll probably heal in three weeks. But your grandma's broken wrist could take eight weeks to heal.

# HOW MANY BONES?

How many bones do you have in your body right now? It's hard to say.

When you were born, you had more than three hundred bones. But since then, some of them have fused, or grown together.

Everyone knows that some kids grow faster than others. Well, some kids' bones fuse earlier, too. That means there's no way of knowing how many bones you have right now.

When you're all grown up, you'll have 206 bones in your body. More than half of them will be in your hands and feet, but your **skeleton** will also include:

22 bones in your skull

26 bones in your spine

24 bones in your rib cage

3 bones in each arm

3 bones in each leg

3 bones in each ear

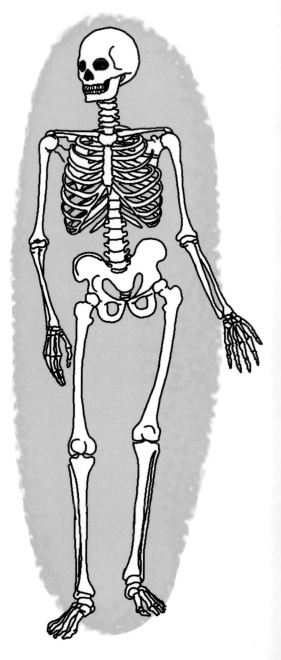

Bones are five times stronger than steel, but they don't weigh as much as you might think. Your skeleton makes up only about 16 percent of your body's total weight.

## Blue-Ribbon Bones

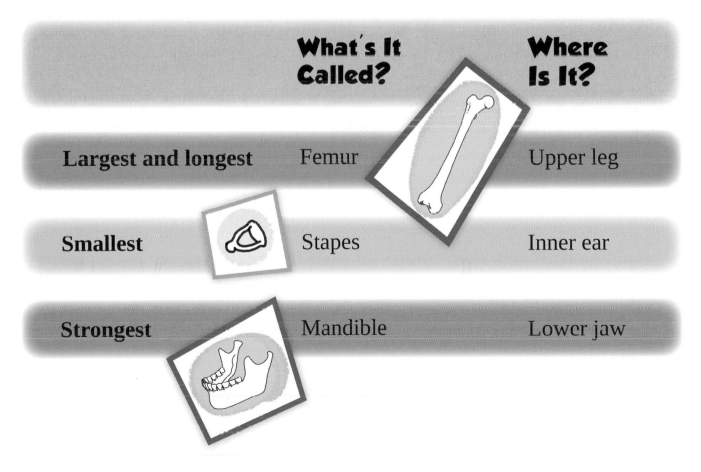

| | What's It Called? | Where Is It? |
| --- | --- | --- |
| **Largest and longest** | Femur | Upper leg |
| **Smallest** | Stapes | Inner ear |
| **Strongest** | Mandible | Lower jaw |

# BENDING BONES

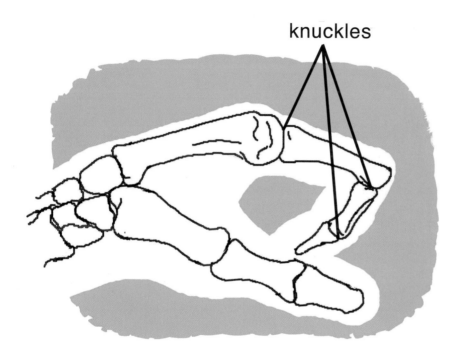

knuckles

Make a fist. Now open your hand. Simple, right? But it wouldn't be if you didn't have knuckles. A knuckle is one of the places where your fingers bend. Each of your fingers has three knuckles. They are some of the more than 230 **joints**—places where two bones meet—in your body.

Knuckles act like door hinges so your fingers can move back and forth. Joints in your knees and elbows work the same way. Neck joints help you turn your head. And shoulder joints let your arms swing in circles.

Some people like to "crack" their joints. Are you one of them?

**Ligaments help hold bones together.**

When you pull on a knuckle or other joint, the pressure inside it drops. Your **ligaments**—the bands of tissue that stretch across joints—get sucked in. And tiny air bubbles form in the liquid that fills the space between bones.

What causes the spine-chilling sound you hear when you crack a joint? Nobody knows. Is it ligaments snapping back into place? Or vibrations caused by bursting air bubbles? Maybe one day scientists will figure it out.

## Bizarre Bending

Can you bend your thumbs or fingers in any direction? People might say you're double-jointed, but that's not really true. It just means your joints are extra flexible.

# NO BONES ABOUT IT

Humans aren't the only animals with hard, bony skeletons. Snakes and squirrels have them. So do mice and monkeys, frogs and flamingoes, turtles and trout.

But some fish have softer, more flexible skeletons. Their skeletons are made of **cartilage**—the same material that gives your ears and nose their shape.

Cartilage might not seem like the best choice for a body frame. But consider this: Fish with softer skeletons—sharks, skates, and rays—have thrived on Earth for 300 million years. They were around long before the dinosaurs, and they're still with us today.

What's the secret to their success? Size. Most ocean predators won't attack larger creatures. And a lightweight skeleton allows sharks, skates, and rays to grow larger without making their bodies too heavy to swim.

**A stingray.**

A whale shark.

# Ocean Giants

The eight largest fish in the world all have skeletons made of cartilage. Whale sharks are the biggest fish of all. They can grow to be as long as a school bus and weigh as much as two elephants.

Ocean sunfish are the largest bony fish. They're a little smaller than a Volkswagen Beetle, and they weigh about half as much as an elephant.

An ocean sunfish.

# SHAPE AND STRUCTURE

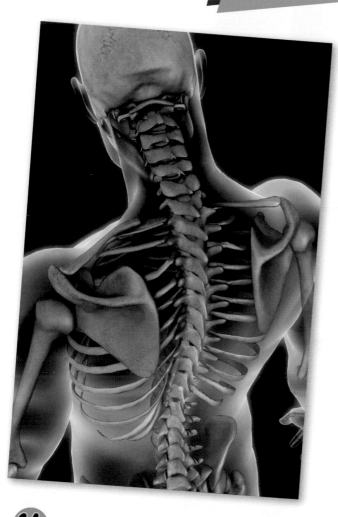

Imagine what you'd look like if you didn't have bones. You'd be nothing more than a puddle of skin and guts heaped on the floor.

That's because your bones do more than move you around. They support your body and give you your shape. They also protect your most important **organs**.

- Your **spine**, or backbone, is made of twenty-six ring-shaped bones that hold your body upright. It also protects your **spinal cord**, a bundle of **nerves** that relays messages between your brain and the rest of your body.

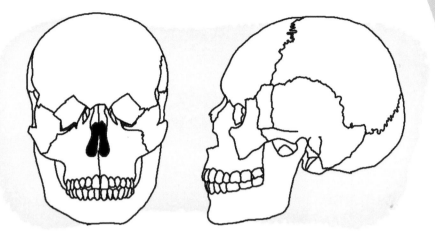

- The twenty-two bones that make up your skull act like a hard, protective helmet for your brain.
- Your heart and lungs are important, too. Luckily, you've got ribs to keep them safe. Most people are born with twenty-four **ribs**, but some people have twenty-two or twenty-six.

**After a good night's sleep, you always wake up a little bit taller.**

## Fact or Fibula?

You're taller in the morning than you are at bedtime. It's a fact. During the day a force called **gravity** pushes down on your body, and the bones in your spine smoosh together. But as you sleep lying down, the spaces between the bones in your spine increase. So by morning, you're about 0.5 inches (1.2 centimeters) taller.

# INSIDE-OUT ANIMALS

Quick—name three animals. Now name three more.

Chances are all six of those animals have skeletons inside their bodies—just like you. But believe it or not, more than 97 percent of all the animals on Earth have **exoskeletons**—hard, protective coverings on the outsides of their bodies. These animals are called **invertebrates**.

Hedgehogs may be small, but they have skeletons inside, just like you.

Insects are invertebrates. So are spiders and lobsters and worms and snails.

Why are invertebrates so easy to overlook? Because most of them are small.

Ever been attacked by an 8-foot (24-meter) spider? Of course not, and here's why: the larger an invertebrate grows, the thicker and heavier its exoskeleton gets. A giant spider's exoskeleton would weigh so much, the spider wouldn't be able to move an inch.

## Stretch and Split

As you grow, so do your bones. But an exoskeleton never changes.

What does an invertebrate do when it outgrows its exoskeleton? It **molts**. The animal's insides press against the hard outer covering until it splits open. Then the little creature wriggles out with a new exoskeleton already in place.

Most insects molt four to eight times while they're growing up. But a lobster molts forty-four times before its first birthday!

# THE BONE ZONE

Think about the last time you ate fried chicken. What do you remember about the bones?

Dead bones are dry and brittle. That's probably why *skeleton* comes from a Greek word that means "dried up."

But living bones are a little bit soft and springy. That's why they can absorb the pressure you put on them when you bat a ball or jump out of a tree.

Most of the bones in your body contain two kinds of tissue. Hard, dense **compact bone** is made up of rings of **minerals**. Below that is a softer layer full of tiny holes. It's called **spongy bone**.

Compact bone

Spongy bone

You already know that bones help you move and protect soft body parts. But you depend on them for other things, too.

- Without the three itty-bitty bones inside each ear, you couldn't hear a thing.
- The long bones in your arms and legs have hollow centers. The soft, squishy **bone marrow** crammed inside them is constantly cranking out a fresh supply of blood cells.
- Bones all over your body store minerals that come from the foods you eat. Without minerals, your muscles couldn't contract and your nerves couldn't carry messages.

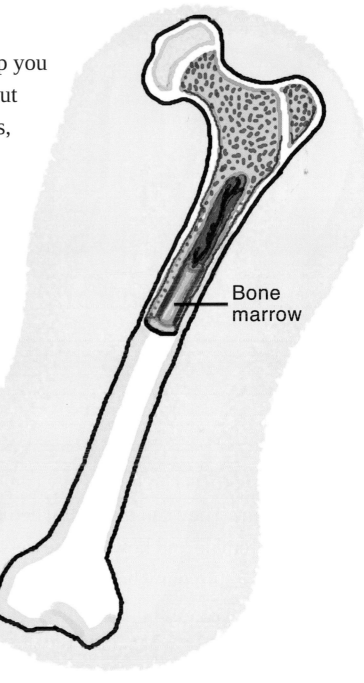

Bone marrow

# BONES TELL TALES

Some scientists spend their whole lives studying bones—and not just living ones. When police find human bones, they want to know who they belonged to and how the person died.

Scientists can help. They can calculate the person's height and weight. They can also tell whether the bones came from a male or a female and how old the person was. Sometimes they can even figure out where the person lived and what kind of job he or she had. And if the bones show injuries, scientists may be able to determine when and how the person died. All these clues help police identify the body and solve the crime.

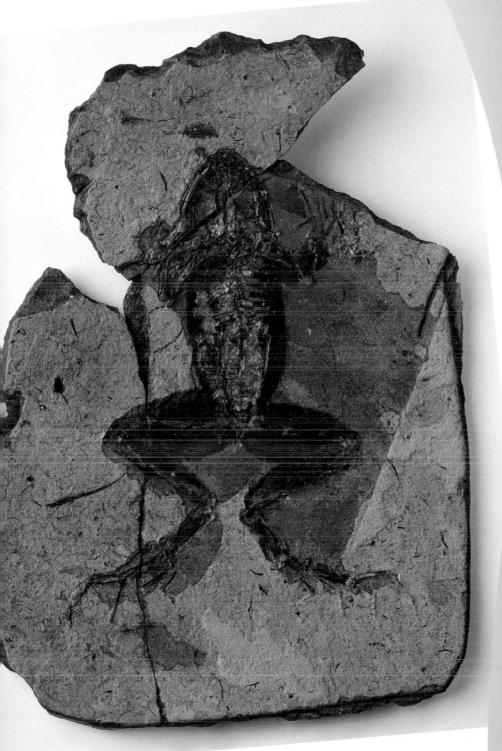

Frog fossil.

# Tales of the Past

When an animal dies, it's usually eaten by a predator. Sometimes its body slowly rots away. But once in a while, a dead creature is quickly buried by ash, sand, or mud. Then, if the conditions are just right, its bones turn into fossils.

By carefully piecing together fossilized bones, scientists can sometimes build part—or even all—of an animal's skeleton. Once they know an ancient animal's size and shape, they may be able to figure out how it lived and what it ate.

# MUSCLE MAKEUP

What does a flame-broiled burger have in common with a tender pork chop and a chicken nugget? They're all made of the same thing—muscle.

The muscles inside your body look a lot like a thick, juicy steak. Look closely at a flank steak, and you'll see that it's made of many long, stringy fibers. So are your muscles. Each of those fibers is a cell.

Most cells are so small that you need a microscope to see them, but not muscle cells. They're as thin as a hair, but they can be up to 12 inches (30 cm) long.

Each muscle cell contains dozens of long, thin **myofibrils**. And each myofibril contains two kinds of proteins—**actin** and **myosin**.

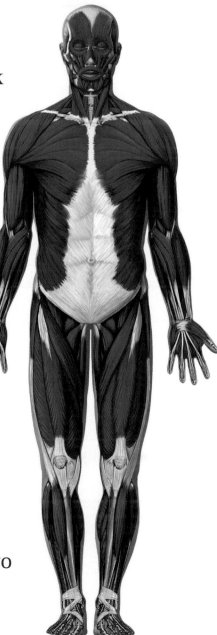

This woman's body weight is made up of mostly muscle.

# The Wonders of Water

Most of your body is made of water, and your muscles are no exception. They're about 75 percent water and 20 percent protein.

# Pump It Up!

The more you use your muscles, the bigger, stronger, and heavier they get. If you're a couch potato, your muscles probably make up about one-third of your body's total weight. But if you play sports every day, they could make up half of your total weight.

# CONTRACTION
# ACTION

Your teacher asks a question, and you know the answer. Almost instantly, your arm shoots up in the air. Then the teacher calls on you, and your arm falls back to your side.

Raising your hand seems pretty easy, right? You probably do it all the time. But let's take a closer look.

First, your ears hear the teacher's question, and your brain processes the sounds. When you realize you know the answer, your brain sends out a message to the nerves in your arm. The nerves tell your muscles to contract, or shorten.

Inside your muscle's myofibrils, hundreds of thin actin filaments slide over thick myosin filaments until they overlap. Each movement is tiny, but together, they create enough force to pull your arm bones high over your head.

When the teacher calls on you, your brain sends your arm another message. As the actin and myosin filaments pull away from one another, your muscles relax and your arm drops down.

## Burly Bands

Muscles aren't attached directly to bones. **Tendons** run between them. These strong, stretchy bands of tissue put the spring in your step and the flick in a frog's tongue.

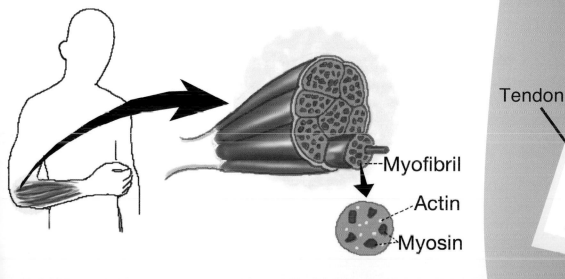

Myofibril

Actin

Myosin

Tendon

# UNDER YOUR
# CONTROL

Every time you raise your hand, pick up a pencil, kick a soccer ball, wiggle you nose, or stick out your tongue, you think about it first. That's because the **skeletal muscles** controlling all these movements are attached to bones, and you decide when to move them.

It's easy to guess what the skeletal muscles in your arms and legs do, but what about the muscles in other parts of your body?

- Your neck muscles rotate your head back and forth, up and down. They also hold your head high.
- Your back muscles keep you standing tall. And they provide the power you need to lift and push objects.
- Your strong, flat belly muscles protect the soft organs of your digestive system.
- The muscles just below your belly let you bend forward and lean to the side.

## Tugging Teams

Most skeletal muscles work in teams. Try lifting and lowering your arm right now. First, one group of muscles pulls your arm up. Then, a second group of muscles pulls your arm back down. The two groups of muscles are like two groups of people battling it out in a tug-of-war match.

# LET'S FACE IT

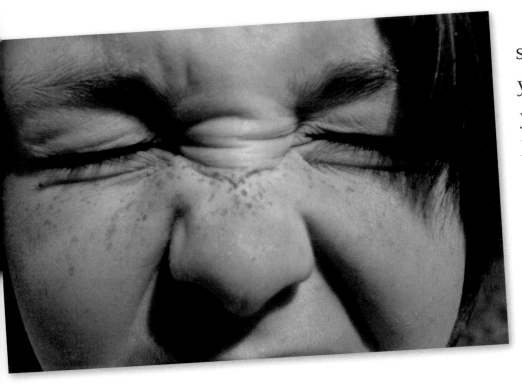

When something stinks, you wrinkle your nose. When your sister tells a lie, you raise one eyebrow. When the sun is too bright, you squint your eyes. When you want to whistle a tune, you purse your lips.

Think of all the ways you move your face every day. Believe it or not, you have more than a hundred skeletal muscles in your head.

Six muscles work together to move your eyeballs up and down, right and left. And more muscles inside your eyeballs help you see.

Muscles inside your nose sniff sweet scents—and nasty ones, too. And when you have a cold, they blow out slimy snot and crusty boogers.

Dozens of muscles take turns contracting and relaxing to tell other people how you feel. You use them to smile, scowl, and frown; to look scared or surprised; and to make goofy faces.

Muscles around and inside your mouth help you, too. You use them to talk, chew food, and stick out your tongue.

## Record-Setting Muscles

| | What's It Called? | Where Is It? |
|---|---|---|
| **Largest and Thickest** | Gluteus maximus | Butt |
| **Smallest** | Stapedius | Inner ear |
| **Longest** | Sartorius | Upper leg |

# TERRIFIC TONGUES

Your tongue is a group of skeletal muscles attached to bone at just one end. That's why you can stick it out and wiggle it around. You need your tongue to talk and eat, but other animals use their tongues in all kinds of ways.

An anteater's long, lean tongue is perfect for catching ants and termites inside its underground nest.

As a snake flicks its tongue, it collects tiny particles from the air. When it rubs the particles into two tiny holes on the roof of its mouth, the snake can smell and taste its surroundings.

A woodpecker keeps its supersized tongue in a groove that wraps around the inside of its skull. When the woodpecker drills holes in trees, its fleshy tongue pads its brain.

How does a gecko clean its eyes? With its tongue!

How does an alligator snapping turtle lure its prey? By wiggling a wormlike structure on the tip of its tongue.

A penguin's tongue has tiny spikes that point backward, toward its throat. The spikes prevent slippery fish from sliding out of the bird's mouth.

When a blue-tongued skink feels scared, it opens its mouth and sticks out its tongue. The shocking colors are usually enough to scare off a predator.

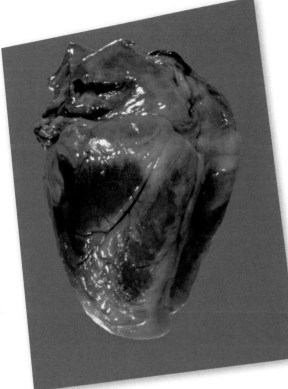

While you're awake, your skeletal muscles are always ready for action. And every night they get a much-needed rest.

But your hardworking heart never takes a break. The fist-sized lump of **cardiac muscle** beats about eighty times a minute day and night, year after year. You don't even have to think about it.

During your lifetime your heart will beat about 3 billion times and pump about 100 million gallons (379 million liters) of blood into your **blood vessels**. From there the layers of **smooth muscle** lining your blood vessels take over. Each time they contract,

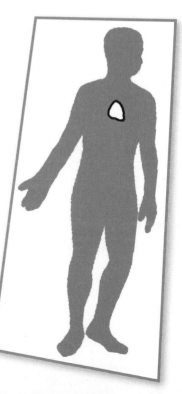

**This illustration shows the location of the heart inside the body.**

blood surges forward on its 60,000-mile (97,000-kilometer) journey through your body.

First, the blood whizzes through your **arteries**, traveling at 1 foot (0.3 meters) per second. But then it puts on the brakes as it squeezes through your superslender **capillaries**. Finally, your blood slowly slogs its way back to your heart through your **veins**.

## Where's the Blood?

Right now your body contains about 6 quarts (5.7 l) of blood. About 24 percent of that blood is in your arteries. About 66 percent is in your veins, and about 10 percent is in your capillaries.

# AIR IN, AIR OUT

Take a deep breath. Now let it out.

You don't have to think about breathing. It just happens. Whenever your cells need a fresh supply of oxygen, your brain sends a message to the smooth muscles inside your chest.

Your **diaphragm** drops down, pulling air into your nose and mouth.

Your **intercostal** muscles lift your ribs up and out.

As your chest expands, air rushes into your lungs and blows them up like balloons.

Then your diaphragm relaxes and moves up.

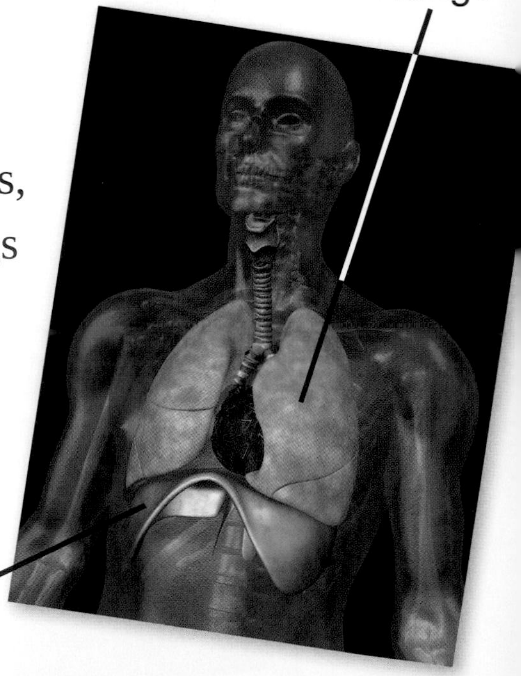

lungs

diaphragm

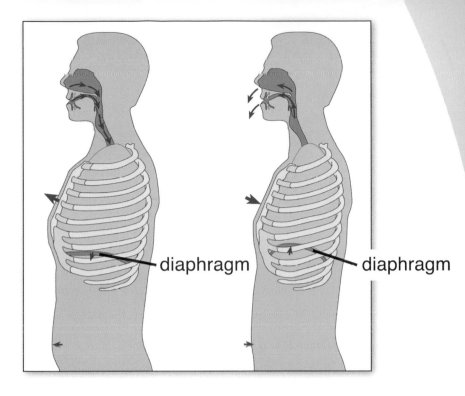

diaphragm

diaphragm

Your intercostal muscles push your ribs down and in.

As your chest shrinks, your lungs collapse, pumping air up and out of your body.

You usually breathe about twelve times a minute. And each breath delivers about 2 cups (0.5 l) of air to your lungs. That works out to 96 gallons (363 l) per hour and 2,300 gallons (8,706 l) per day. That's a lot of air!

## Diaphragm Distress

Most of the time your diaphragm moves smoothly, up and down. But if you eat too much or too fast, it may lose its rhythm. As it jerks and jolts, you suck in air so suddenly that your **vocal cords** snap, producing a loud "hic." Yup, you've got the hiccups.

# DOWN THE HATCH

Ever watched yourself eat? Give it a try. Grab a snack and head for the nearest mirror.

Sure, chewing with your mouth open is kind of gross. But it's the best way to understand how **digestion** begins.

As your teeth chomp and grind, your tongue muscles roll the mangled mash into a soft, moist ball. Then they push it to the back of your throat.

As you swallow, rings of smooth muscle in your **esophagus** contract in waves, pushing food toward your stomach. It's just like what happens when you squeeze a tube of toothpaste.

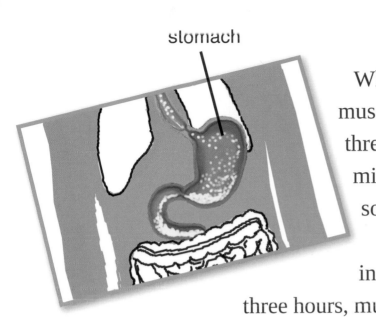

stomach

When your stomach is full, its strong muscular walls start contracting about three times a minute. They squeeze, mix, and churn the food into a thick, soupy mixture.

After the food has been in your stomach for about three hours, muscles push it into your small intestines. Then the nutrients in the food move into your bloodstream.

large intestine

small intestine

About six hours later the undigested leftovers move into your large intestine. Muscles squeeze water out of the waste, forming brown lumps of poop.

But it will be another eighteen hours before you feel the urge to go to the bathroom. After the wastes pass out of your body, take a look in the toilet. Can you see any traces of the snack you ate?

# GEE WHIZ!

HA HA HA HA HA HA HA HA HA

Ever laughed so hard you peed in your pants? Muscles were to blame.

Pee, or urine—as doctors and scientists call it—is a pale yellow liquid. It's made of water, salts, and all kinds of chemicals.

Your body is constantly cranking out a steady stream of urine. It's produced in two fist-size organs called **kidneys**. They're located near the middle of your back, just below your ribs. More than 50 gallons (189 l) of blood flow through your kidneys every day. As the bean-shaped organs clean your blood,

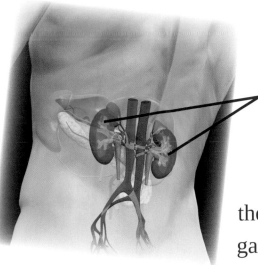

Kidneys

they filter out about 0.5 gallons (1.9 l) of water and waste products.

The urine trickles down two tubes and empties into your **bladder**.

When your bladder is full, your body tells you it's time to pee. That's when you head for the bathroom. As soon as you're ready, a ring of smooth muscle below your bladder relaxes, and urine flows out.

Sometimes when you laugh really hard, your bladder muscles relax a little bit, and a few drops of urine dribble out. Don't feel bad. It happens to almost everyone.

## Out of Control

When babies are born, they can't control their bladder muscles. That's why they have to wear diapers.

# SHIVER AND SHAKE

Like dogs and ducks, parrots and porcupines, you're a **warm-blooded** animal. That means your body always stays the same temperature—about 98.6 degrees Fahrenheit (37 degrees Celsius).

Check out the average annual temperatures of these American cities:

| | |
|---|---|
| Fargo, North Dakota | 41˚F (5˚C) |
| Boston, Massachusetts | 51˚F (10˚C) |
| Orlando, Florida | 72˚F (22˚C) |
| Phoenix, Arizona | 73˚F (23˚C) |

**The average body temperature of a dog is about 101°F (38°C).**

Not one of them is as warm as your body. So where do you get the heat you need to live and grow? From your muscles. As you walk and talk, blink and breathe, your muscles contract. And that produces heat—lots of it.

But if you go outside on a cold day or swim in chilly water, your body may have trouble staying warm. Then your brain tells muscles all over your body to contract and relax very quickly.

All those tiny movements make you shiver and shake. Your teeth chatter when your jaw muscles respond. Goose bumps spread up your arms as muscles in your skin get to work. In just a few minutes you feel toasty warm.

From warming us up and protecting our organs to controlling our every move, it's hard to believe all the ways bones and muscles help us every day. And we aren't alone. Many other animals depend on them, too.

# GLOSSARY

**actin**—A thin protein filament in muscles.

**artery**—A blood vessel that carries blood away from the heart.

**bladder**—The organ that holds urine made in the kidneys.

**blood vessel**—A tube that carries blood throughout the body.

**bone marrow**—A soft squishy material inside some bones. It makes blood cells.

**capillary**—A tiny blood vessel through which oxygen and nutrients move into cells and carbon dioxide moves into blood.

**cardiac muscle**—The muscle that makes up the heart.

**cartilage**—The flexible material that forms the skeletons of some fish. Cartilage also gives your nose and outer ears their shape.

**compact bone**—The hard, outer layer of bone. It contains minerals.

**diaphragm**—A sheet of muscles that forms the floor of the chest cavity.

**digestion**—The process of breaking down food.

**esophagus**—The tube that connects the pharynx and stomach.

**exoskeleton**—The rigid outer covering of some invertebrates.

**gravity**—A force that pulls on objects. Earth's gravity makes objects on or near Earth fall toward the center of the planet.

**intercostal muscle**—A muscle located between a pair of ribs.

**intestine**—The part of the digestive system that breaks down food particles and allows nutrients to pass into the blood. It's often divided into the small intestine and large intestine.

**invertebrate**—An animal without a backbone or internal skeleton.

**joint**—The place where two bones meet.

**kidney**—A fist-sized, bean-shaped body organ that filters waste materials out of the blood.

**lever**—A simple tool consisting of a rigid bar that pivots around a fulcrum when force is applied.

**ligament**—A band of tissue that stretches across a joint.

**mineral**—A chemical that comes from food and helps various body parts do their jobs.

**molt**—To shed an old outer covering that is worn out or too small.

**myofibril**—Long, thin structures inside muscle cells. They contain actin and myosin filaments.

**myosin**— A thick protein filament in muscles.

**nerve**—A bundle of cells that carry messages to and from the brain.

**nutrient**—A substance that keeps the body healthy. It comes from food.

**organ**—A body part made up of several kinds of tissue that work together. The heart is an organ. So are the stomach and lungs.

**oxygen**—An invisible gas that animals need to live.

**rib**—One of the bones that surrounds and protects the chest cavity.

**skeletal muscle**—A muscle that an animal can move at will. Most skeletal muscles are attached to and pull on a bone.

**skeleton**—The collection of bones that support and shape the body.

**smooth muscle**—Muscle that lines the walls of the organs. Its movements can not be actively controlled.

**spinal cord**—A bundle of nerves protected by the spine. It relays messages between the brain and nerves all over the body.

**spine**—Backbone; the twenty-six bones that run down the middle of the back.

**spongy bone**—The soft, lightweight, inner layer of bone. It is full of holes.

**tendon**—A band of strong, stretchy tissue that joins muscles to bones.

**vein**—A blood vessel that carries blood toward the heart.

**vocal cord**—A flap of tissue in the larynx that plays a role in producing the voice.

**warm blooded**—Having a body temperature that stays the same no matter how cold or warm it is outside.

# A NOTE ON SOURCES

Dear Readers,

After learning the basics about muscles and bones in medical text books, I started hunting for some fun facts in popular magazines and medical journals. That's where I learned how muscles help us breathe, stay warm, digest food, pee, and poop.

It was tougher to find information about the muscles and bones of other animals, but I slowly collected tidbits like the number of muscles in a caterpillar's body, why invertebrates are usually so small, and all the ways animals use their tongues.

Then I met an osteologist (a doctor who studies bones) at a friend's party. He suggested that I discuss why people are a little taller in the morning and why it's impossible to say how many bones a kid has.

Finally, at the end of my research process, I spoke with a forensic anthropologist about the techniques he uses to study bones and how his findings help police.

—Melissa Stewart

# FIND OUT MORE

## BOOKS

Brynie, Faith Hickman. *101Questions About Muscles: To Stretch Your Mind and Flex Your Brain.* Minneapolis, MN: Twenty-First Century Books, 2007.

Seuling, Barbara. *Your Skin Weighs More Than your Brain and Other Freaky Facts About your Skin, Skeleton, and Other Body Parts.* Mankato, MN: Picture Window Books, 2008.

## WEBSITES

**Get Body Smart: Muscule Tutorials and The Skeletal System**
This site contains text and diagrams that give a complete overview of your muscles and bones.
www.getbodysmart.com/ap/muscularsystem/menu/menu.html

**Get Body Smart: The Skeletal System**
This site contains text and diagrams that give a complete overview of your bones.
www.getbodysmart.com/ap/skeletalsystem/skeleton/menu/animation.html

**Kids Health**
This site answers just about any question you might have about your body and keeping it healthy.
http://kidshealth.org/kid/

# INDEX

Page numbers in **bold** are illustrations.

## ABOUT THE AUTHOR

**Melissa Stewart** has written everything from board books for preschoolers to magazine articles for adults. She is the award-winning author of more than one hundred books for young readers. She serves on the board of advisors of the Society of Children's Book Writers and Illustrators and is a judge for the American Institute of Physics Children's Science Writing Award. Stewart earned a B.S. in biology from Union College and an M.A. in science journalism from New York University. She lives in Acton, Massachusetts, with her husband, Gerard. To learn more about Stewart, please visit her website: www.melissa-stewart.com.

## ABOUT THE ILLUSTRATOR

**Janet Hamlin** has illustrated many children's books, games, newspapers, and even Harry Potter stuff. She is also a court artist. The Gross and Goofy Body is one of her all-time favorite series, and she now considers herself the factoid queen of bodily functions. She lives and draws in New York and loves it.